STRUM IT GUITAR

AUTHENTIC CHORDS
ORIGINAL KEYS
COMPLETE SONGS

BEST OF THE doors

CONTENTS

Cover photography: © Doors Photo Archive

ISBN 0-634-00217-1

HAL•LEONARD®
CORPORATION

7777 W. BLUEMOUND RD. P.O. BOX 13819 MILWAUKEE, WI 53213

Visit Hal Leonard Online at
www.halleonard.com

HOW TO USE THIS BOOK

Strum It!™ is the series designed especially to get you playing (and singing!) along with your favorite songs. The idea is simple—the songs are arranged using their original keys in *lead sheet* format, giving you the chords for each song, beginning to end. The melody and lyrics are also shown to help you keep your spot and sing along.

Rhythm slashes are written above the staff as an accompaniment suggestion. Strum the chords in the rhythm indicated. Use the chord diagrams found at the top of the first page of the arrangement for the appropriate chord voicings.

Additional Musical Definitions

⊓	• Downstroke
V	• Upstroke
D.S. al Coda	• Go back to the sign (𝄋), then play until the measure marked *"To Coda,"* then skip to the section labelled *"Coda."*
D.C. al Fine	• Go back to the beginning of the song and play until the measure marked *"Fine"* (end).
cont. rhy. sim.	• Continue using similar rhythm pattern.
N.C.	• Instrument is silent (drops out).
𝄆 𝄇	• Repeat measures between signs.
1. 2.	• When a repeated section has different endings, play the first ending only the first time and the second ending only the second time.

Love Me Two Times

Words and Music by The Doors

Additional Lyrics

3. Love me one time, could not speak.
   Love me one time, baby,
   Yeah, my knees got weak.
   Love me two times, girl,
   Last me all through the week.
   Love me two times, I'm goin' away.

Been Down So Long

Words and Music by The Doors

Additional Lyrics

2. I said, warden, warden, warden,
   Won't you break your lock and key?
   I said, warden, warden, warden,
   Won't you break your lock and key?
   Hey, come along here, mister,
   C'mon, and let the poor boy be.

4. Baby, baby, baby,
   Won't you get down on your knees?
   Baby, baby, baby,
   Oh, won't you get down on your knees?
   C'mon, little darlin',
   C'mon, ah, give your love to me. Oh, yeah.

Blue Sunday

Words and Music by The Doors

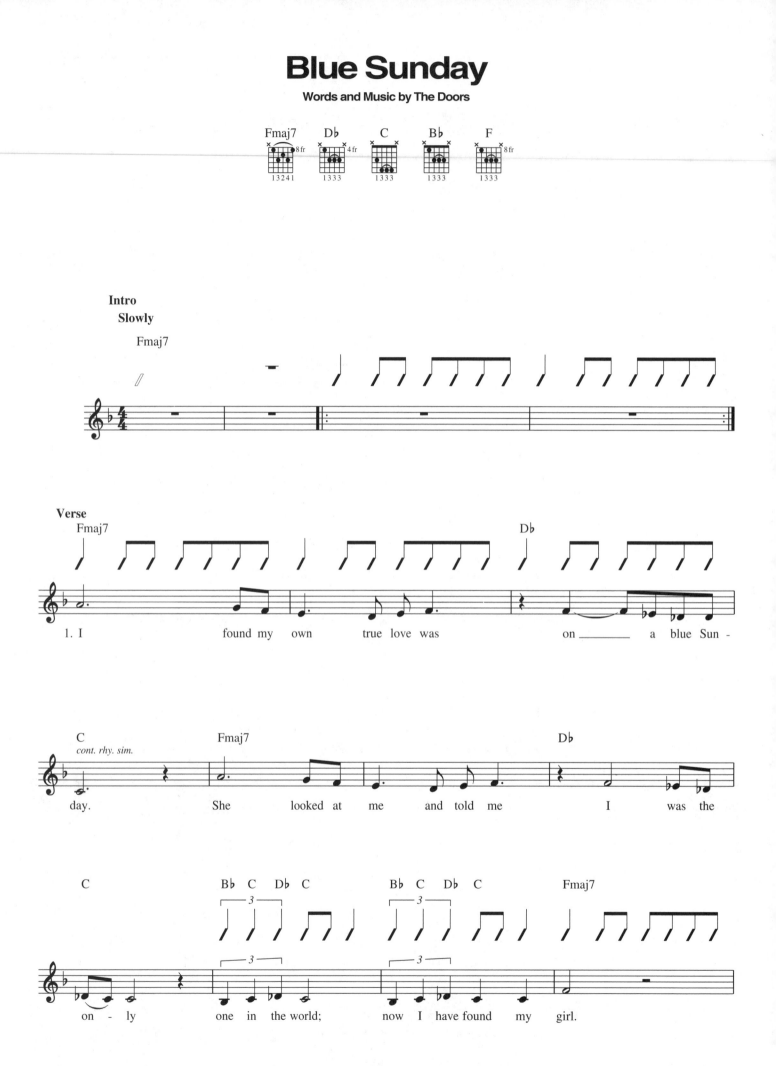

Break on Through
(To the Other Side)

Words and Music by The Doors

Em   D

Intro
Moderately Fast

Em   *play 4 times*

1. You know the

Verse

Em

day de - stroys the night, _   night di - vides the day; _
2., 3., 4. *See Additional Lyrics*

D   *cont. rhy. sim.*   Em

tried to run,   tried to hide.   Break on   through _ to the oth - er side, _

1.

To Coda 1
To Coda 2

break on   through _ to the oth - er side, _   break on   through _ to the oth - er side, _ yeah.

2.

2. We

Keyboard Solo
Em

Interlude
Em   *play 8 times*

Ev - 'ry - bod - y _____   loves ___ my

Additional Lyrics

2. We chased our pleasures here,
   Dug our treasures there,
   But can you still recall the time we cried?
   Break on through to the other side,
   Break on through to the other side.

3. I found an island in your arms,
   A country in your eyes,
   Arms that chain, eyes that lie.
   Break on through to the other side,
   Break on through to the other side,
   Break on through, ow! Oh, yeah!

4. Made the scene from week to week,
   Day to day, hour to hour,
   The gate is straight, deep and wide.
   Break on through to the other side,
   Break on through to the other side.

Cars Hiss by My Window

Words and Music by The Doors

Additional Lyrics

3. Window started trembling with a sonic boom.
   Window started trembling with a sonic boom, boom.
   A cold girl will kill you in a darkened room.

Crystal Ship

Words and Music by The Doors

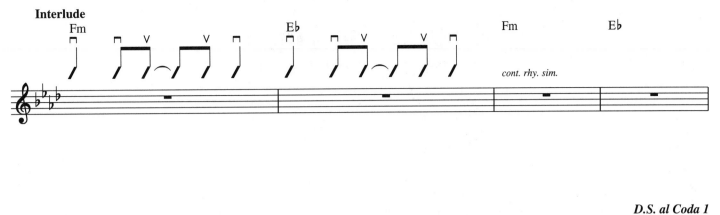

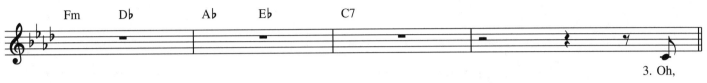

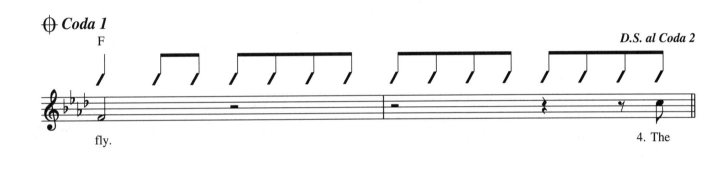

Additional Lyrics

2. The days are bright and filled with pain.
   Enclose me in your gentle rain,
   The time you ran was too insane,
   We'll meet again, we'll meet again.

3. Oh, tell me where your freedom lies,
   The streets are fields that never die,
   Deliver me from reasons why
   You'd rather cry, I'd rather fly.

4. The crystal ship is being filled,
   A thousand girls, a thousand thrills,
   A million ways to spend your time;
   When we get back, I'll drop a line.

End of the Night

Words and Music by The Doors

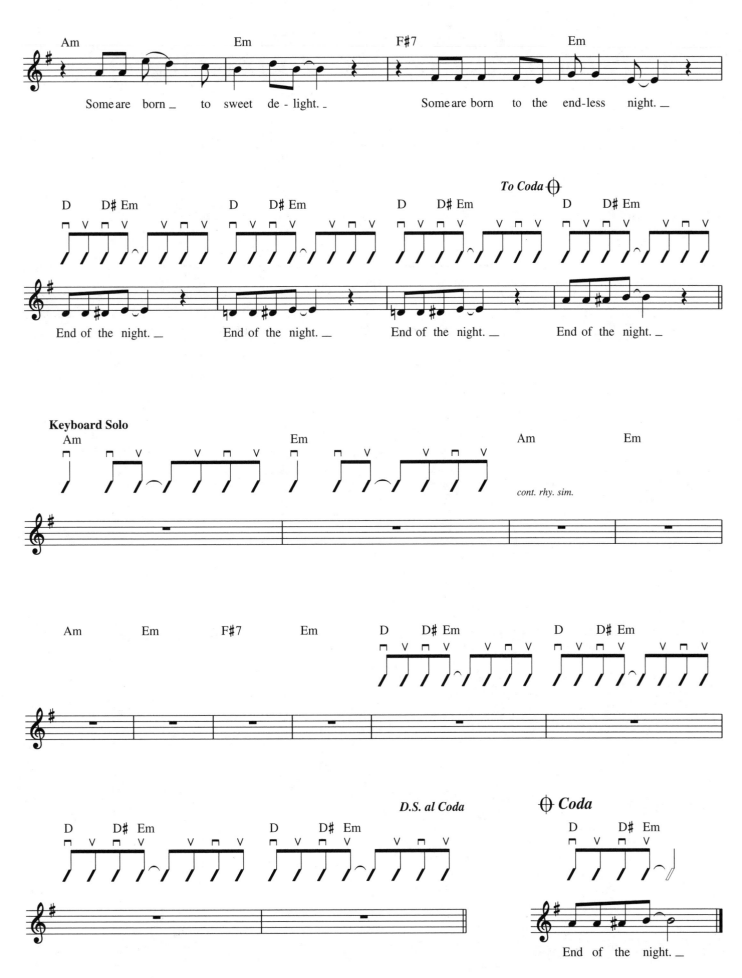

End of the night. _

Hello, I Love You
(Won't You Tell Me Your Name?)

Words and Music by The Doors

Additional Lyrics

2. She holds her head so high
   Like a statue in the sky.
   Her arms are wicked and her legs are long.
   When she moves my brain screams out this song.

Hyacinth House

Words and Music by The Doors

I Looked at You

Words and Music by The Doors

Additional Lyrics

2. I walk with you,
   You walk with me.
   I talked to you,
   You talked to me.

L.A. Woman

Words and Music by The Doors

Mis-ter Mo - jo ris - in'. _____ Mo - jo ris - in'. _____

Got my Mo - jo ris - in'. _____ Mis-ter Mo - jo ris - in' _____

got to keep on ris - in'. _____ Ris - in', ris - in', _____

ris - in', ris - in', _____ ris - in', ris - in', _____

ris - in', ris - in', _____ ris - in', ris - in', __

Guitar Solo
A Tempo

C   D   A   *D.S. al Coda*

cont. rhy. sim.

4. Well, I

Coda

A   G

___ cit - y of night, __   cit - y of night. __

A

Outro
w/ Voc. ad lib.

Repeat and Fade

A

L. A. ___ wom - an,   L. A. ___ wom - an.

Light My Fire

Words and Music by The Doors

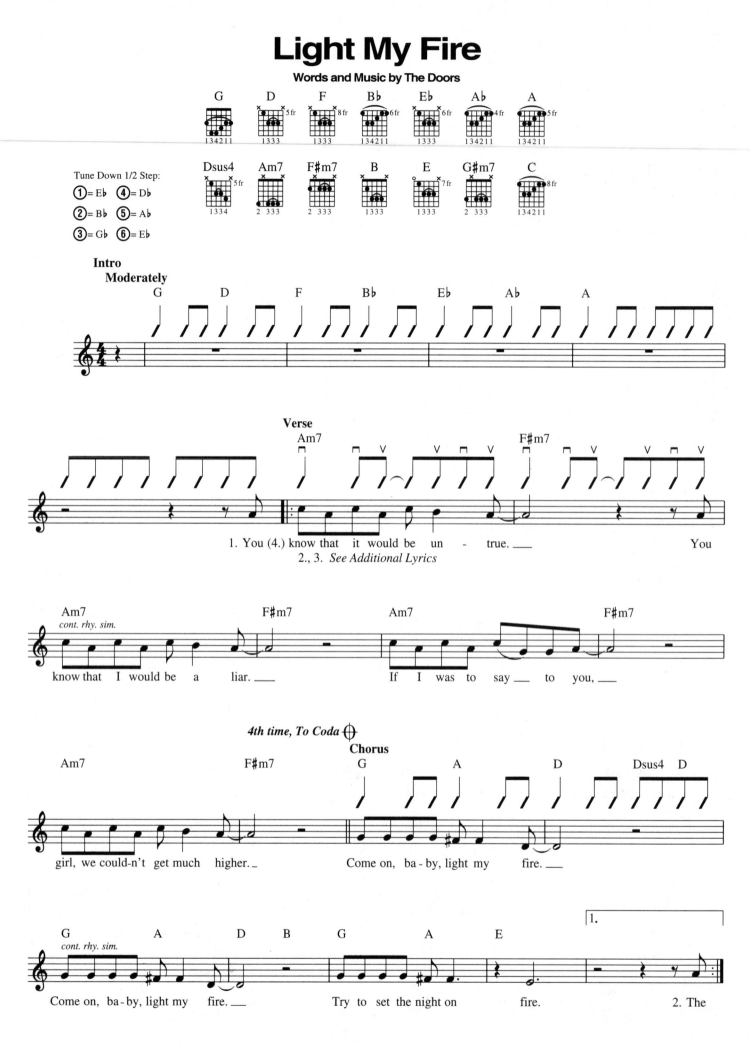

Additional Lyrics

2., 3. The time to hesitate is through,
No time to wallow in the mire.
Try now we can only lose,
And our love become a fun'ral pyre.

Love Her Madly

Words and Music by The Doors

Love Street

Words and Music by The Doors

My Eyes Have Seen You

Words and Music by The Doors

Additional Lyrics

2. My eyes have seen you.
   My eyes have seen you.
   My eyes have seen you turn and stare,
   Fix your hair, move upstairs,
   Move upstairs, move upstairs.

3. My eyes have seen you.
   My eyes have seen you.
   My eyes have seen you free from disguise,
   Gazing on a city under television skies,
   Television skies, television skies.

People Are Strange

Words and Music by The Doors

Tell All the People

Words and Music by The Doors

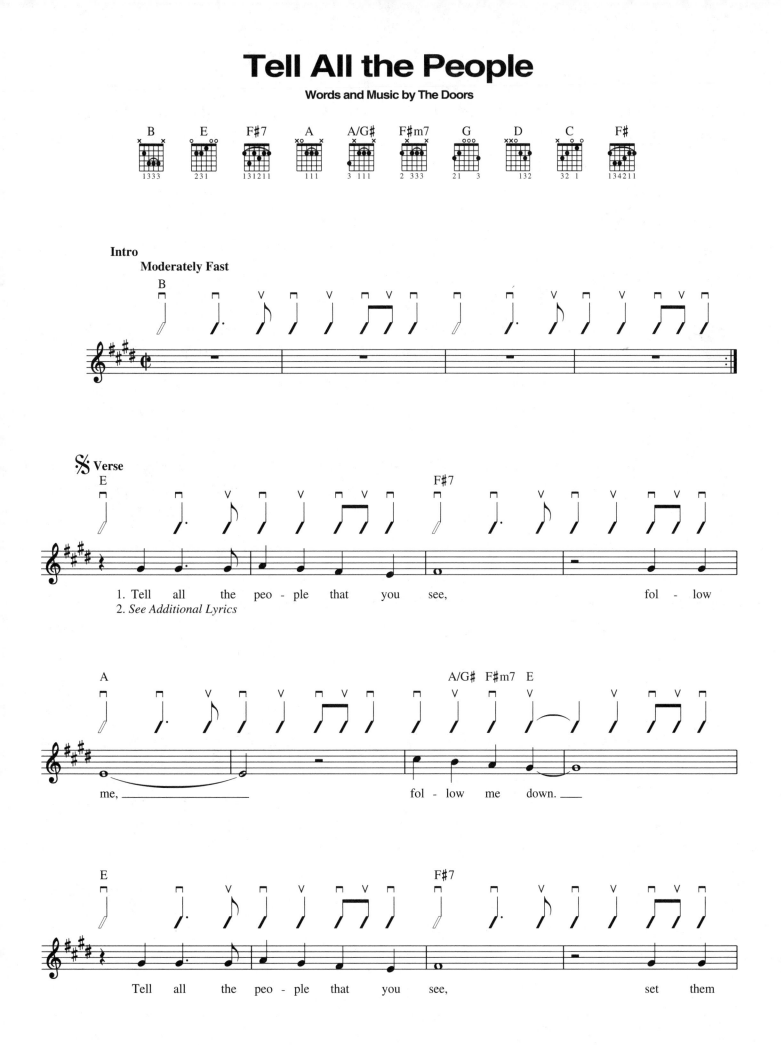

Additional Lyrics

2. Can't you see the wonder at your feet,
   You're life's complete.
   Follow me down.
   Can't you see me growing,
   Get your guns, the time has come
   To follow me down.

Queen of the Highway

Words and Music by The Doors

Additional Lyrics

2. Now they are wedded, she is a good girl;
   Naked as children out in the meadow,
   Naked as children, wild as can be.
   Soon to have offspring,
   Start it all over.
   Start it all over.

3. American boy, American girl,
   Most beautiful people in the world!
   Son of a frontier Indian swirl,
   Dancing thru the midnight whirl-pool.
   Formless. Hope it can continue a little while longer.

Riders on the Storm

Words and Music by The Doors

If you give this man a ride, sweet fam - i - ly will die. Kill - er on the road.

1. 2. 3.

4. Girl, you

Keyboard Solo
Em   D   Em   D   Em   D

play 24 times

last time, D.S. al Coda

Interlude
Em

play 4 times

Em

⊕ *Coda*

Guitar Solo   **Outro**
Em   Em

play 4 times

Rid - ers on the storm, __ rid - ers on the storm, __

Repeat and Fade

__ rid - ers on the storm, __ rid - ers on the storm. __

Additional Lyrics

4. Girl, you gotta love your man.
Girl, you gotta love your man.
Take him by the hand,
Make him understand.
The world on you depends,
Our life will never end.
Gotta love your man.

Roadhouse Blues

Words and Music by The Doors

Additional Lyrics

2. Yeah, in back of the roadhouse they got some bungalows.
   Yeah, in back of the roadhouse they got some bungalows.
   And that's for the people who like to go down slow.

4. When I woke up this mornin' I got myself a beer.
   When I woke up this mornin' I got myself a beer.
   The future is uncertain and the end is always near.

Soul Kitchen

Words and Music by The Doors

Strange Days

Words and Music by The Doors

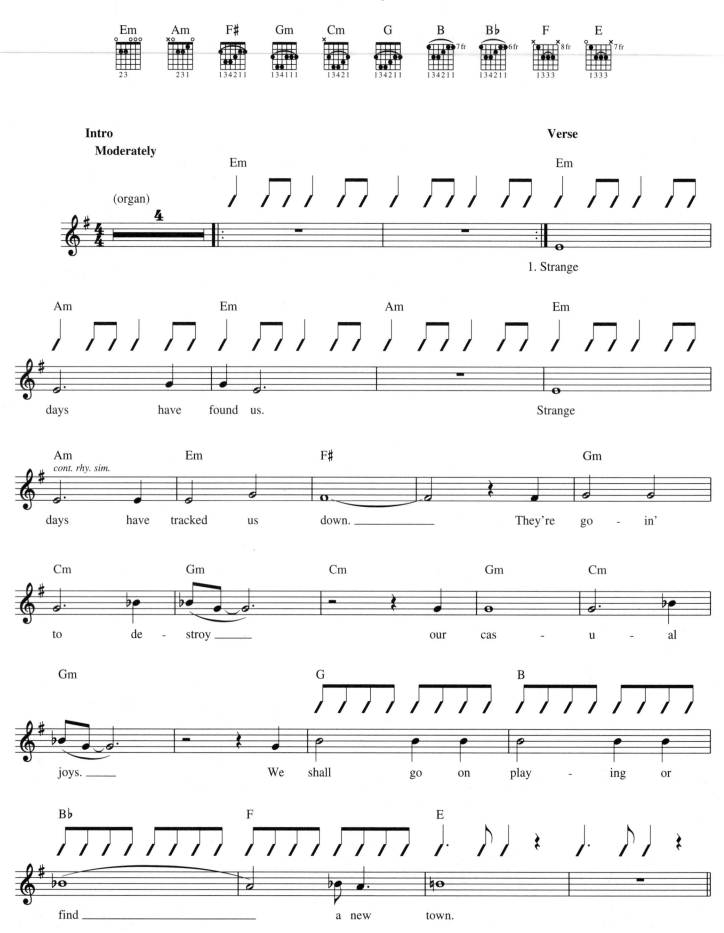

*Strum chord as rapidly and
continuously as possible.

Additional Lyrics

3. Strange days have found us.
   And through their strange hours
   We linger alone,
   Bodies confused,
   Memories misused.
   As we run from the day
   To a strange night of stone.

Summer's Almost Gone

Words and Music by The Doors

Take It As It Comes

Words and Music by The Doors

3. Go real slow, you'll like it more and more.

Take it as it comes. Spe - cial - ize in hav - in' fun. ___

D.S. al Coda

Coda

mov - in' much too fast. Mov - in' much too fast.

Mov - in' much too fast. _____

Additional Lyrics

2. Time to walk;
   Time to run.
   Time to aim your arrows at the Sun.

Touch Me

Words and Music by The Doors

Twentieth Century Fox

Words and Music by The Doors

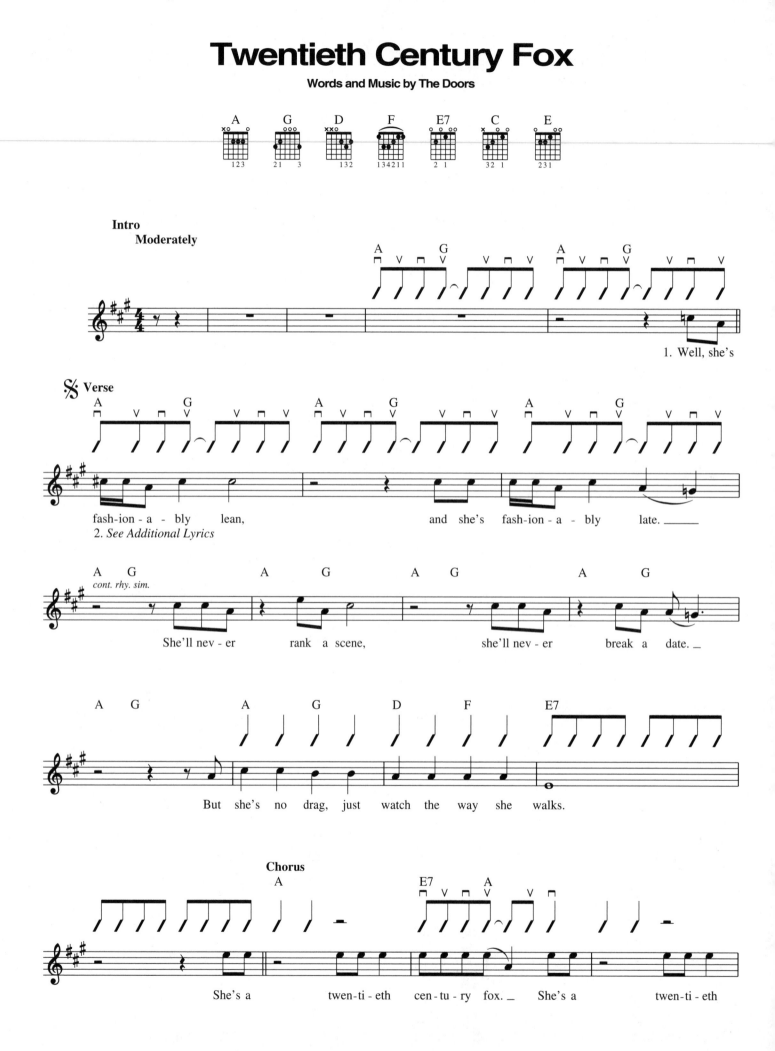

1. Well, she's

fash-ion-a-bly lean, and she's fash-ion-a-bly late. _____
2. *See Additional Lyrics*

She'll nev-er rank a scene, she'll nev-er break a date. _

But she's no drag, just watch the way she walks.

She's a twen-ti-eth cen-tu-ry fox. _ She's a twen-ti-eth

Additional Lyrics

2. She's the queen of cool,
   And she's the lady who waits.
   Since her mind left school,
   It never hesitates.
   She won't waste time on element'ry talk.

Wintertime Love

Words and Music by The Doors

Intro

Waltz

1. Win - ter - time winds blow cold this sea - son,
2. *See Additional Lyrics*

fall - in' in love I'm hop - in' to be. Wind is so

cold is that the rea - son, keep - ing you warm, your

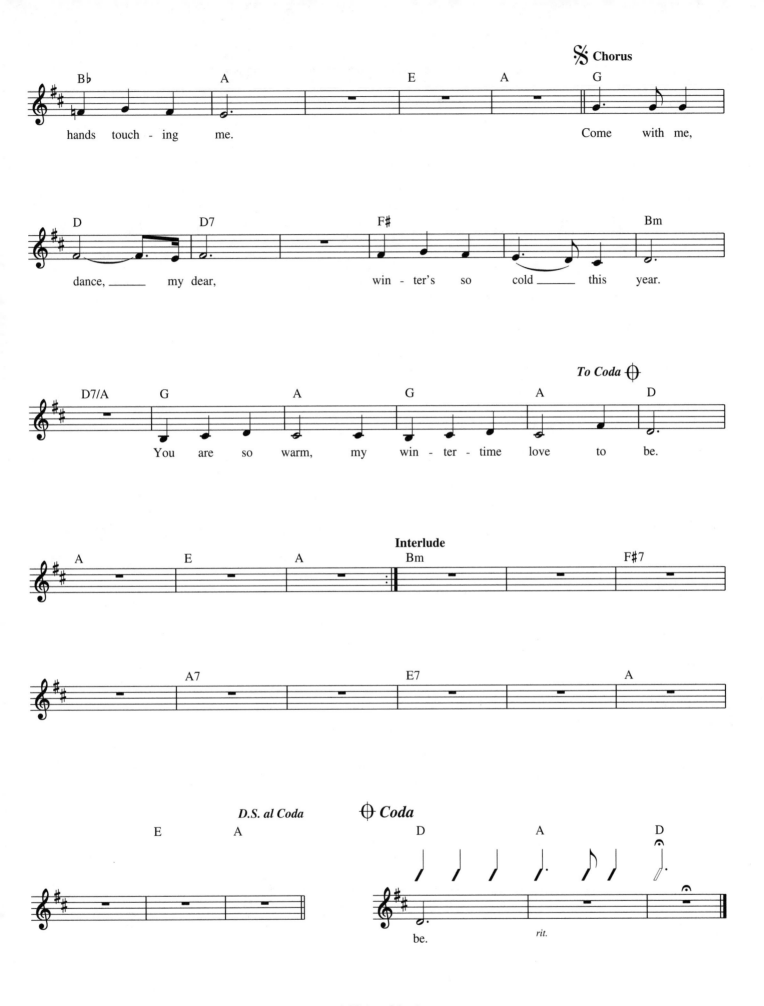

Additional Lyrics

2. Wintertime winds, blue and freezin',
   Comin' from northern storms in the sea.
   Love has been lost, is that the reason,
   Trying desperately to be free.

Yes, the River Knows

Words and Music by The Doors

Wishful Sinful

Words and Music by The Doors

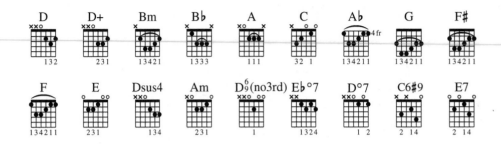

Intro

Moderately

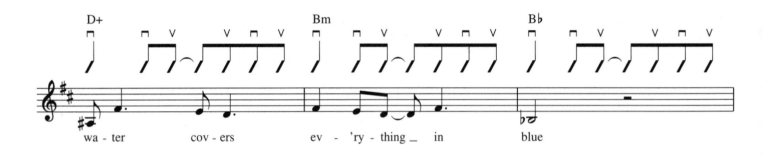

Wish - ful _____ sin - ful,

wa - ter cov - ers ev - 'ry - thing _ in blue

cool - ing wa - ter.   1., 3. Wish - ful _____ sin - ful,

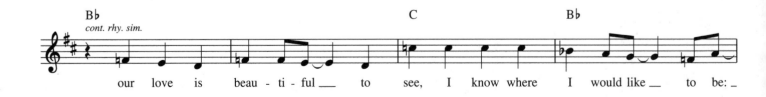

our love is beau - ti - ful _ to see, I know where I would like _ to be: _

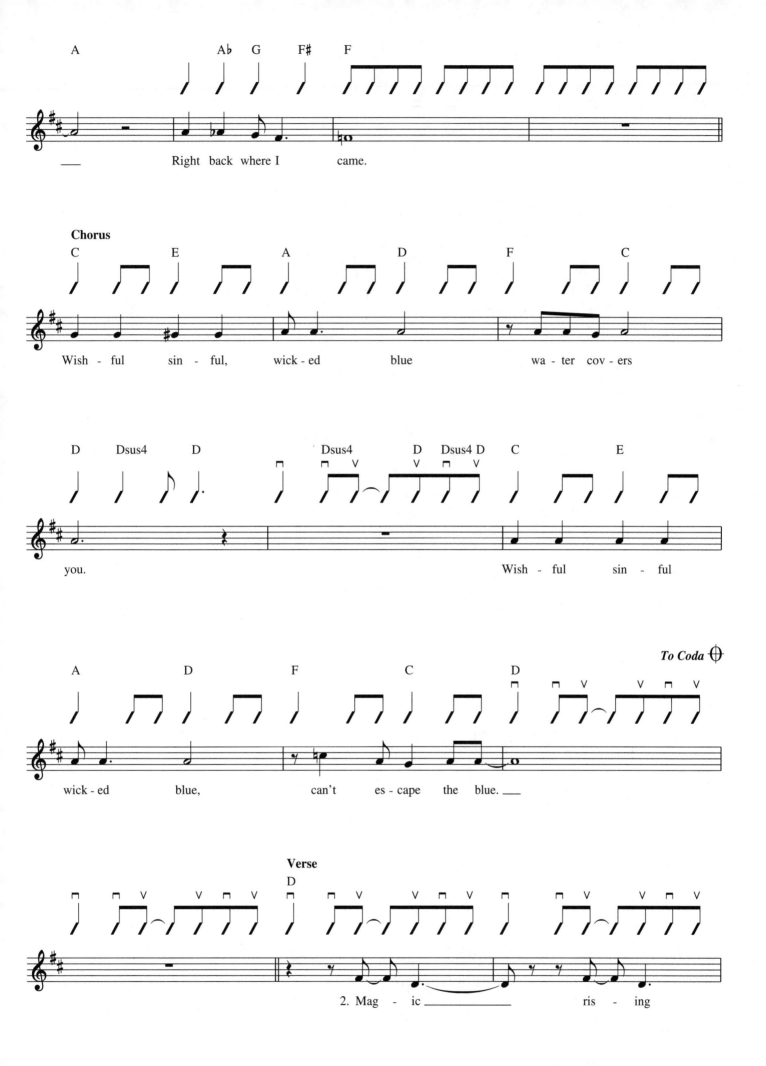